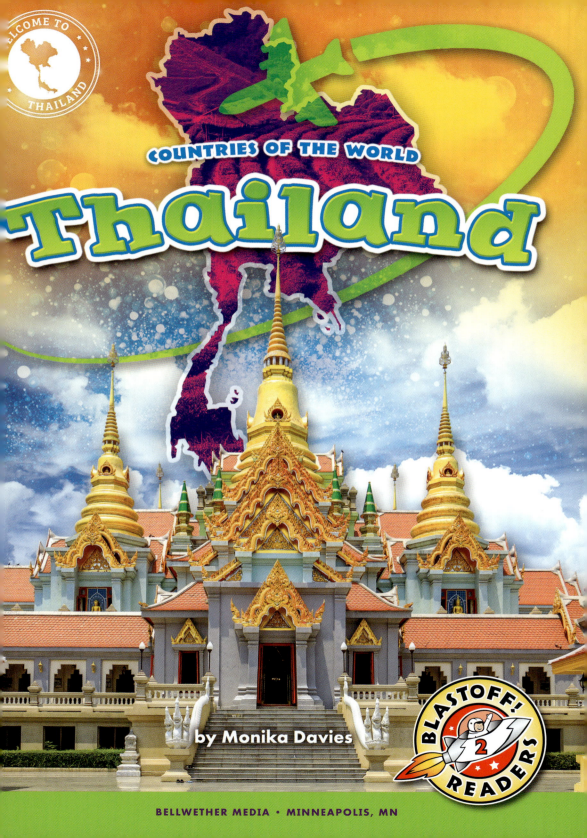

Blastoff! Readers are carefully developed by literacy experts to build reading stamina and move students toward fluency by combining standards-based content with developmentally appropriate text.

LEVELS

Level 1 provides the most support through repetition of high-frequency words, light text, predictable sentence patterns, and strong visual support.

Level 2 offers early readers a bit more challenge through varied sentences, increased text load, and text-supportive special features.

Level 3 advances early-fluent readers toward fluency through increased text load, less reliance on photos, advancing concepts, longer sentences, and more complex special features.

★ **Blastoff! Universe**

Reading Level

Grade K

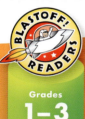
Grades 1–3

Grade 4

This edition first published in 2024 by Bellwether Media, Inc.

No part of this publication may be reproduced in whole or in part without written permission of the publisher. For information regarding permission, write to Bellwether Media, Inc., Attention: Permissions Department, 6012 Blue Circle Drive, Minnetonka, MN 55343.

Library of Congress Cataloging-in-Publication Data

Names: Davies, Monika, author.
Title: Thailand / by Monika Davies.
Description: Minneapolis : Bellwether Media, Inc., 2024. | Series: Blastoff! Readers: Countries of the world | Includes bibliographical references and index. | Audience: Ages 5-8 | Audience: Grades 2-3 | Summary: "Relevant images match informative text in this introduction to Thailand. Intended for students in kindergarten through third grade"– Provided by publisher.
Identifiers: LCCN 2023003625 (print) | LCCN 2023003626 (ebook) | ISBN 9798886874341 (library binding) | ISBN 9798886876222 (ebook)
Subjects: LCSH: Thais–Juvenile literature. | Thailand–Juvenile literature.
Classification: LCC DS563.5 .D38 2024 (print) | LCC DS563.5 (ebook) | DDC 915.9304–dc23/eng/20230127
LC record available at https://lccn.loc.gov/2023003625
LC ebook record available at https://lccn.loc.gov/2023003626

Text copyright © 2024 by Bellwether Media, Inc. BLASTOFF! READERS and associated logos are trademarks and/or registered trademarks of Bellwether Media, Inc.

Editor: Rebecca Sabelko   Designer: Gabriel Hilger
Printed in the United States of America, North Mankato, MN.

Table of Contents

All About Thailand	4
Land and Animals	6
Life in Thailand	12
Thailand Facts	20
Glossary	22
To Learn More	23
Index	24

All About Thailand

Bangkok

Thailand is in Southeast Asia. Its capital is Bangkok.

Thailand is one of the most visited countries in the world. It is known for its **temples** and beaches.

Land and Animals

Mountains rise in the north and west. The Chao Phraya River flows through the central **plains**.

A **plateau** covers the east. Sandy beaches line the southern shores.

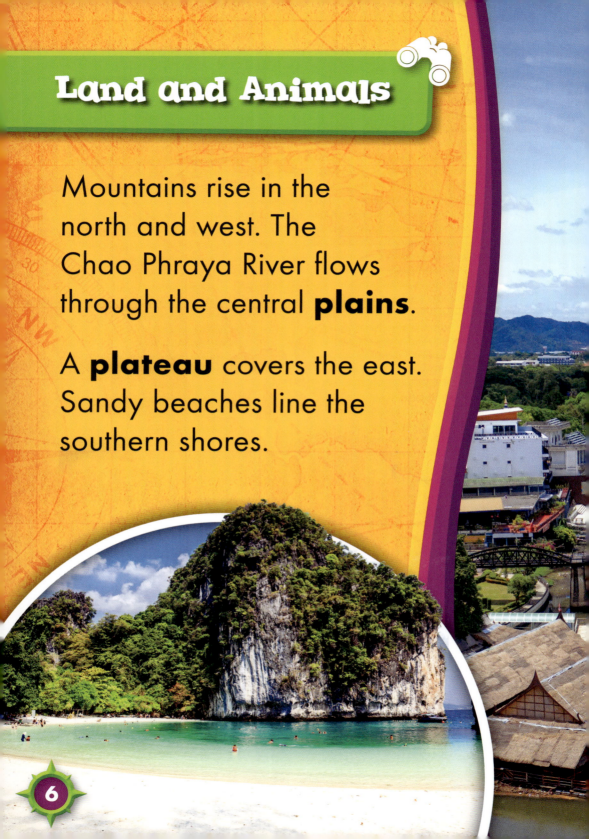

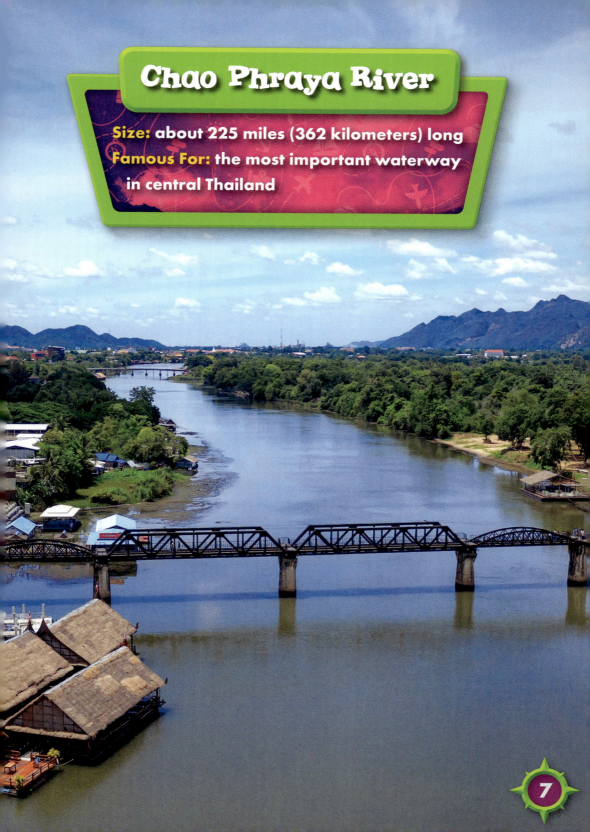

Chao Phraya River

Size: about 225 miles (362 kilometers) long
Famous For: the most important waterway in central Thailand

monsoon flood

Monsoons control the **climate**. These winds change direction every season.

Spring is hot and dry.
Summer is hot and rainy.
Winter is cooler and dry.

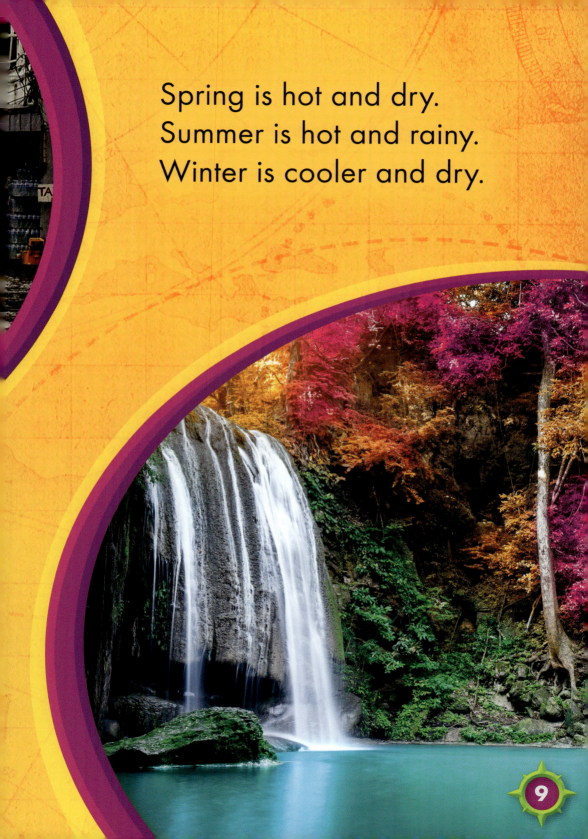

Clouded leopards hunt in forests. Gibbons swing in the trees.

lar gibbons

Animals of Thailand

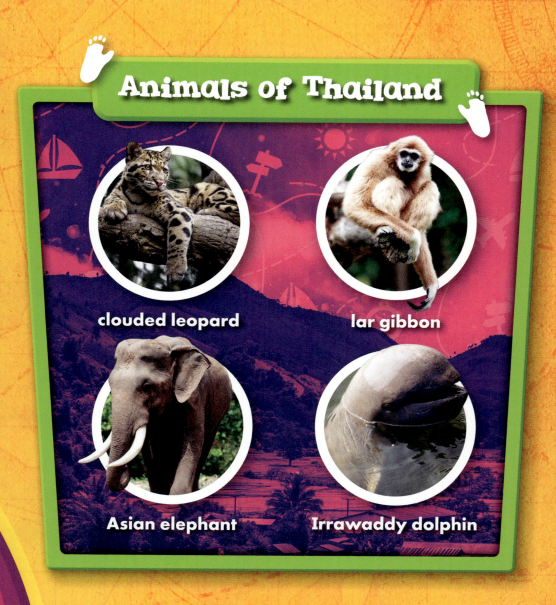

clouded leopard

lar gibbon

Asian elephant

Irrawaddy dolphin

Elephants live in national parks. Dolphins swim near coasts.

Life in Thailand

Most people live in cities. Bangkok is the largest city.

Most people speak Thai. Nearly all people practice **Buddhism**. They visit temples called wats.

Wat Thang Sai

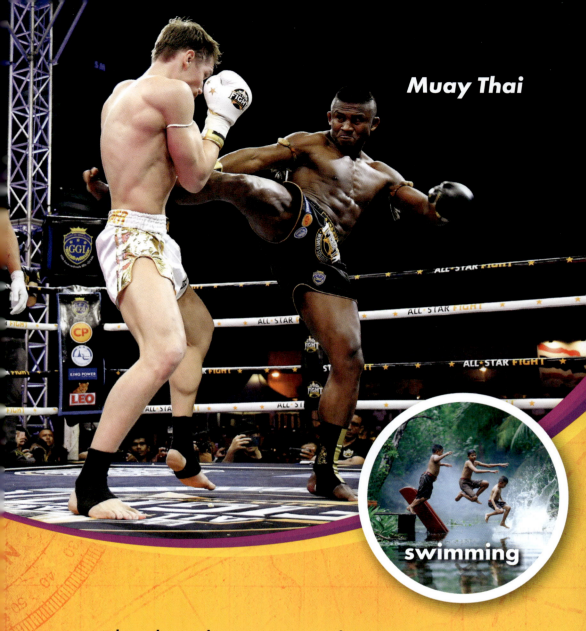

Muay Thai

swimming

Thailand's national sport is *Muay Thai*. It is a **martial art**. People also enjoy swimming.

People like to fly kites in spring.

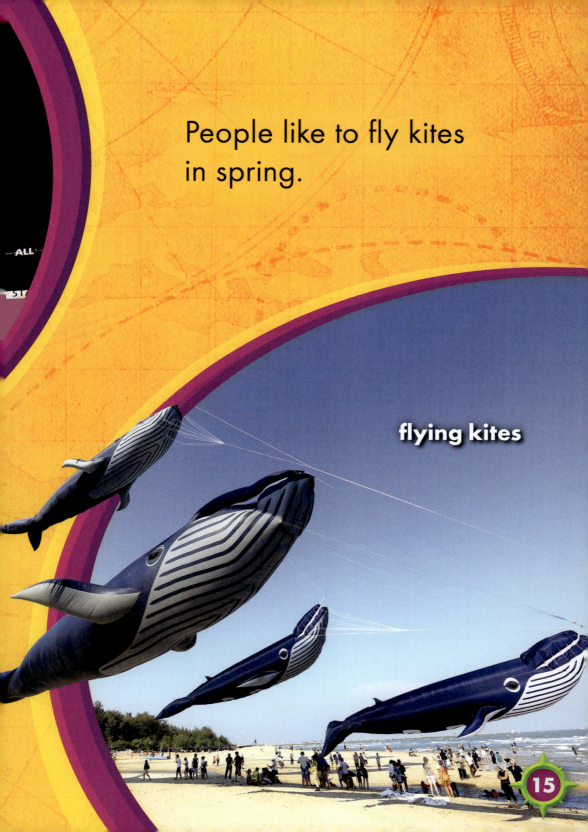

flying kites

pad thai

Pad thai is a popular dish of fried noodles. *Gaeng keow wan* is a green curry. *Som tam* is a spicy papaya salad.

Kluai khaek are sweet, deep-fried bananas!

Thai Foods

pad thai

gaeng keow wan

som tam

kluai khaek

Buddhists honor *Visakha Bucha* Day. They help others in need.

Songkran

Songkran is the Thai New Year. People spray water at each other for good luck. They come together to **celebrate**!

Thailand Facts

Size:
198,117 square miles
(513,120 square kilometers)

Population:
69,648,117 (2022)

National Holiday:
Birthday of King Vajiralongkorn (July 28)

Main Language:
Thai

Capital City:
Bangkok

Famous Face

Name: Tony Jaa

Famous For: Thai martial artist, actor, director, and more

Religions

Muslim: 4%
Christian: 1%
Buddhist: 95%

Top Landmarks

Damnoen Saduak Floating Market

Huay Mae Khamin Waterfall

Wat Phra Kaew

21

Glossary

Buddhism—a religion of eastern and central Asia based on the teachings of Buddha, the founder of Buddhism

celebrate—to do something special or fun for an event, occasion, or holiday

climate—the usual weather conditions in a certain place

martial art—a style and technique of fighting and self-defense that is practiced as sport

monsoons—winds that change direction each season; monsoons can bring heavy rain.

plains—large areas of flat land

plateau—a flat, raised area of land

temples—buildings used for religious purposes

To Learn More

AT THE LIBRARY

Bennington, Clara. *Grand Palace*. Minneapolis, Minn.: Jump!, 2020.

Mather, Charis. *A Visit to Thailand*. Minneapolis, Minn.: Bearport Publishing, 2023.

Spanier, Kristine. *Thailand*. Minneapolis, Minn.: Jump!, 2020.

ON THE WEB

Factsurfer.com gives you a safe, fun way to find more information.

1. Go to www.factsurfer.com.
2. Enter "Thailand" into the search box and click 🔍.
3. Select your book cover to see a list of related content.

Index

animals, 10, 11
Bangkok, 4, 5, 12
beaches, 5, 6
Buddhism, 12, 18
capital (see Bangkok)
Chao Phraya River, 6, 7
cities, 12
climate, 8
coasts, 11
flying kites, 15
food, 16, 17
forests, 10
map, 5
monsoons, 8
mountains, 6
Muay Thai, 14
national parks, 11
people, 12, 14, 15, 19
plains, 6

plateau, 6
say hello, 13
Songkran, 19
Southeast Asia, 4
spring, 9, 15
summer, 9
swimming, 14
temples, 5, 12
Thai, 12, 13
Thailand facts, 20–21
Visakha Bucha Day, 18
winter, 9

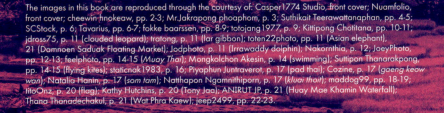

The images in this book are reproduced through the courtesy of: Casper1774 Studio, front cover; Nuamfolio, front cover; cheewin hnokeaw, pp. 2-3; Mr.Jakrapong phoaphom, p. 3; Suthikait Teerawattanaphan, pp. 4-5; SCStock, p. 6; Tavarius, pp. 6-7; fokke baarssen, pp. 8-9; totojang1977, p. 9; Kittipong Chotitana, pp. 10-11; jdross75, p. 11 (clouded leopard); tratong, p. 11 (lar gibbon); toten22photo, pp. 11 (Asian elephant), 21 (Damnoen Saduak Floating Market); Jodphoto, p. 11 (Irrawaddy dolphin); Nakornthia, p. 12; JoeyPhoto, pp. 12-13; feelphoto, pp. 14-15 (*Muay Thai*); Mongkolchon Akesin, p. 14 (swimming); Suttipon Thanarakpong, pp. 14-15 (flying kites); staticnak1983, p. 16; Piyaphun Juntraverot, p. 17 (pad thai); Cozine, p. 17 (*gaeng keow wan*); Natalia Hanin, p. 17 (*som tam*); Natthapon Ngamnithiporn, p. 17 (*kluai thoit*); maddog99, pp. 18-19; titoOnz, p. 20 (flag); Kathy Hutchins, p. 20 (Tony Jaa); ANIRUT JP, p. 21 (Huay Mae Khamin Waterfall); Thana Thanadechakul, p. 21 (Wat Phra Kaew); jeep2499, pp. 22-23.

24